MW01504190

Heaven to Me

Heaven to Me

Abe Louise Young

Abe Louise Young

Headmistress Press

Copyright © 2016 by Abe Louise Young
All rights reserved.

ISBN-13: 978-0692604748
ISBN-10: 069260474X

This book may not be reproduced, in whole or in part, including illustrations, in any form (beyond that permitted by Sections 107 and 108 of the U.S. Copyright Law and except by reviewers for the public press), without written permission from the publishers.

Cover art © 1992 by Sharon Beals. "Tree Swallow, Tatoosh Island." Photographed by Sharon Beals at Cornell University Museum of Vertebrates.

Italicized lines in "Dash" are excerpted from *Open Me Carefully: Emily Dickinson's Intimate Letters to Susan Huntington Dickinson* (Paris Press, 1998).

Cover & book design by Mary Meriam.

The author thanks the editors of the following journals for first publishing these poems:
Bloom: "Ode to alternative insemination"
The Ilanot Review: "Phone book"
Wicked Alice Poetry Journal: "Pollination" (as an earlier version)

PUBLISHER

Headmistress Press
60 Shipview Lane
Sequim, WA 98382
Telephone: 917-428-8312
Email: headmistresspress@gmail.com
Website: headmistresspress.blogspot.com

For Louise, Ocean, Shea and Sunlight

Contents

Arrival

At twelve, I became an astronaut
reaching out with huge gloved hands
and red tunnel vision toward the moon.
The completely full moon, the whole moon
with no end in sight, round abandoned moon,
voluminous milky moon, powder keg, blind crater,
volcano, jumping with cows moon, moon without flag;
I was hungry for the whole cold, distant, unreliable moon, my
lost, longed-for, luscious, silk-lined moon, my unattainable,
faithful, private moon, moon without man, tidal, hovering,
mercurial, tender, trusted moon, menstrual, dream dial
moon; I lumbered toward it night after night in the puffy
white suit, hearing the roar of my own secret heavy
breathing, my eyes smarting, embarassed and
failing until suddenly, floating, pulsing, unable
to rest or breathe or land, in one movement
I reached out and found it:
a live breast in my hand.

Equality hymn

God,
I adore women whose bodies
spill, stretch, round out, roll,
yield, loll, expand, fold
more body than I can grab
onto with my hands or mouth

O yes, to have a very fat lover
is heaven to me, I want her
reading in my bed extravagantly
at any hour, it helps me survive

Lying face-down on my fat woman's body
is floating on soft perpetual truths
and when we sleep, my face
will find her breast, my hands
tuck in, legs grip her hips

To anchor our ardor
we're always accidentally
tantrically rubbing up
tangential to anything, we love
to touch each other

In the ordinary starving world
I see no one diving
for the mons Venus
of wild big angry women

but to lift
a mountain breast
with both my hands is bliss

Looking at my lover,
some people whisper,

She's not healthy,
something is wrong
with her self-esteem...

(We adore her Self lavishly)

What do you see in her?

(She's *so* pretty.
I see power, divinity)

Obese.

(Please)

You're going to die too
and you won't have been living
in a landscape of rippling
wonder unraveling
detractors and
throwing off
flowers
at every
touch

The best first date

We walk into the past, hands
scented with amber resin
and cookstove ash,
into an alder grove
where our female ancestors,
friends and old lovers,
our hags and witches,
viragos and crones,
griots and whistleblowers,
studs, femmes, transfolk,
Furies and the whole
damn House of Atreus
is gathered

in a raucous circle
on pillowy red cushions,
talking about us,
drinking damiana tea
from tiny cups,
revealing no lunacy,
smiling indulgently,
dropping by to enjoy
our liberation and to stop
us from making
early promises.

Ode to alternative insemination

O, how my ovaries start crowing for attention
at any mention of lesbians
having children!

I read the announcement printed on linen,
knock back my fresh-squeezed orange juice
and run into the street with my empty glass—

I know there are fountains of sperm going off
all over the world, it's like Versailles out there, Rococo,
24/7, no monuments needed,

it's sheer geysers, a natural resource,
anonymous,
humble and glorious!

Imagine the plumage in the bathroom stalls,
the public parks! Who needs to pay
doctors for vials in freezers?

My breasts begin to dance
like ecstatic little dogs on their hind legs.
Work it on up, boys, high in the air,

and let me catch some!
Shoot into my front yard,
from Paris, from Dallas, from Dakar, from El Salvador,

from an airplane, a rowboat, a car,
I don't care!
Just let me catch some!

Pollination

A persistent woman can be pollinated, that's why.
I was jealous of my friend, her life, her perfect city,
her gestation—
pregnant by mail.

Her perineum tore & out it slid,
          a universe in a package,
          a universe covered with hair.

The midwife said: Hamburger buns!

       (Translation: It's a girl.)

New stories are coming toward us like 10,000 tornadoes.
The baby was born with a hole in her heart;
everything is ready to burst.

       dehisce (di-HIS), verb

          1. To split open, as the pod of a plant.
             2. To gape.

The heart surgeons run for thread and canvas sails.
Get out of the way! No—
get in!

Transgenerational

Offenders can spot us
in a sea of children:
the smell of sweet saltwater hope
and hidden fear sweat
disguised as pair bonding

My cousin, she often had lice
and never checked her reflection
in the mirror

I was a small filly with a flashing
red light: *already broken in*

Mom couldn't tell
the carpenter not to take us
back into the shed, the shed,
the shed, the shed, the shed
where everything happened
I would kill to forget

And even before his gym teacher
fucked him, I'm sorry,
my brother was a child
burning in dry ice

Mom watched from the kitchen,
dissociative, not equipped
to interrupt, whatever happened,
her own shed in the way,

DNA encoded
from her first abuser
braiding her hair before
each time—
—but please note:

My lesbianism has absolutely
nothing to do with any of this
and if you suggest it does, I'll cut you
out

Phone book

I met Gertrude Stein
by the river Seine
where she was spilling green marbles
down the alleys.

Under my arm I carried a Torah
on a great long roll
of butcher paper—
a phone book Torah,
with names and locations
of the exact 7.2 billion people
alive on the planet today
in no certain order,
every life included
and no name prioritized.

Gertrude and I embraced,
unscrolled the Torah
and read aloud in unison
and drank red wine like hags
and dipped hot baguettes
in butter, and after
we intoned each name
Gertrude did a little dance
and yelled
Encore!

Perfect

Inside me she blossoms
and unfolds

five fingers,
I grip

her wrist,
contract, expand,

she knocks
hello, rocks

in my belly
vibrato

and pulls out
the instant I say so

Thesis defense

You need to choose
between using your ands
or
your ampersands,
he said at the final critique
& climactic finale
of our funded years together.

It's like being good
at embroidery:
you don't want anyone
to see the messy stitches.

I fingered my hem,
stuttered, but aren't
and and *ampersand*
two different words
with different bodies?

And is dependable,
a workhorse, strides
upright and humble,
offers androdgynous quiet
support.

&, on the other hand, lounges
in deep cleavage, strolls
& fucks loudly, holds
each arm out for lost
words to grab onto.

And can be a perfect,
tiny brass safety pin,
but badass bitches
like ampersand are
never invisible
stitches.

Feet

The honored bearded professor
lecturing at the museum
on postlyric poetry said,
The author as a function is dead.
Poetry is not expressed by us, but uses
us to express itself.
A stop, a gap between my belly and throat.
The idea left me listless,
badly kissed.

I rode home thinking,
we don't want to be used,
not as a mop or a dishwasher,
nor registrar, shelter or jester.
Not as a shellfish or potter,
not as a puppet, ink blotter,
vessel, soliloquy, canopy.
We are women with big bodies, reading poetry.
There's clay in the ground,
brown and red, ready for a wheel.
It wants to be shaped into a bowl.
I don't want brains
or professors in my poetry.
I want food and bowls and spoons and feet.

Breakup

I finally
grasped
the essence
of her fury:
she'd barely
grazed

the surface
of my world
yet dreamed
she was fifty
fathoms deep,
told her mother
I was hers
to keep.

And in one long
breath, I left her: a
woman who
    never asked me
questions.

Inferiority complex

The saddest sex
right now is sex
with myself alone,
imagining my ex-wife
making love
to her new wife

I come vicariously
out of my misery
through their happiness
—it's disastrous

Dash

And I do love to run fast — and hide away
from them all: here in dear Susie's bosom
                              —Emily Dickinson

O Emily D., you knew
riding the dash was like lashing
            one log to the next, a river raft for feeling—

        was like lying down on a blanket in the field with Susan,
        time-stealing, kissing, tinkering with iambics,
        tickling her with your feet—

            was joining everything equally, one long breath
            in the transport of her bud—

the dash let you keep writing and talking while part of you
slipped away, planning—
                        a black cake with a folded note

sent down in your pulley and basket,
a lavender, borage, and parsley bouquet
embroidered on her handkerchief,

 a long silence before a night unveiling – tracing,
        taking off the white linen dress, a rainstorm, her hand in
            heat lightning, lacing up your naked back—

            Title divine, is mine.
            The Wife without
            the Sign –

Bad vocab

I have anti-trust
for men or women
who write 85% love poems
and use the word collarbone
with the words butterfly or sip,
who describe their new
girlfriend's breasts as tawny
and their ex-wives' vaginas
as muscular or long

Seriously, fuck any poet
who describes
her ex-wife's
vagina
at all

Muse

You smell like stargazer lilies,
call me *my bed,* scratch
and massage my ticklish head.

You demand my vocabulary
be taut and iambic,
my face enjambed
between your breasts,

my footwork so fancy,
my breathing ecstatic,
my action verbs exact.

O Muse, you are playing with the tether

and my body
will need sewing
back together
again.

Don't decide to die without consulting me

(for queer youth everywhere)

So yes,
some young activists,
artists & queers
lose relatives
in layers
& sometimes
walk around
naked
from stare
to stare.

First, grandparents
resist, then uncles
& fathers
fade, siblings
cease to radio in,
mothers fumble,
anthills rise
over roads
home

but
lily, lady, lad,
lass, listen:
the radio
of love
is on, you're live,
don't go silent yet.

We can fix any
emergency,
you can cocoon,
rewrite the rules,
fuck indiscriminately,
sob or strip in class,
but please don't decide
to die without
consulting me.

Please
inform your friends
& deities,
read runes,
let us feed you
whipped cream
& berries
on a silver
baby spoon,

try
a change
of latitude,
charter a unicorn,
style your hair
with new warrior
attitude,

remember
that in every country,
laundromat,
café, hamlet,
cell or paradise
on earth

someone gorgeous,
someone honest & wonderful
is probably waiting nearby,
idly reading
the funnies,
their heart filled
with peonies,

thumbs hooked
in belt loops, waiting
with a big mysterious
smile to welcome
you home.

Invitation

Lake water's lapping,
my love: lay down your labors,

kiss my lips,
open the flask

of your hips—

About the Author

Abe Louise Young is an independent writer and social justice activist. A native of New Orleans, she now lives in Austin, Texas, where she leads the Revolution Writing Workshop.

Her work has won a Grolier Poetry Prize, the Hawai'i Review's Nell Altizer Prize, a Narrative Magazine Story Prize, and the Academy of American Poets Prize, among others.

She's also the author of *Queer Youth Advice for Educators: How to Respect and Protect Your LGBTQ Students* and a previous chapbook of poetry, *Ammonite*. Both are available for free download at abelouiseyoung.com.

Gratitude

Deep thanks to my poetry teachers Elizabeth Alexander, Ellen Doré Watson, Naomi Shihab Nye, Karl Kirchwey, Arlie Parker, Mary Zimmerman and Khaled Mattawa.

I am forever grateful to friends and mentors Alan Shefsky, Diana Nichols, Paige Schilt, Alan Altimont, Margaret Halpin, Amy Boutell, Sharon Bridgforth, Jenny Browne, Marcela Contreras, Teresa Hall, Luz Guerra, Jesse Bertron, Carrie Fountain, Amy King, Lisa L. Moore, Philip Pardi, Gabrielle Calvocoressi, Marcela Sulak, Alisa Shor, and many others—your brightness lights my way.

Thank you to Sharon Beals for sharing the tree swallow's nest, and to Rebecca Solnit for the gift of space and silent time.

To the women of the Revolution Writing Workshops and to Mary Meriam, Rita Mae Reese and Risa Denenberg at Headmistress Press—thank you.

For resources, time and faith in my work, I'm grateful to The Beinecke Foundation, the James Michener Center for Writers and the Poetry Center at Smith College.

Headmistress Press Books

Tiger Laughs When You Push
Ruth Lehrer

Night Ringing
Laura Foley

Paper Cranes
Dinah Dietrich

A Crown of Violets
Renée Vivien tr. Samantha Pious

On Loving a Saudi Girl
Carina Yun

The Burn Poems
Lynn Strongin

I Carry My Mother
Lesléa Newman

Distant Music
Joan Annsfire

The Awful Suicidal Swans
Flower Conroy

Joy Street
Laura Foley

Chiaroscuro Kisses
G.L. Morrison

The Lillian Trilogy
Mary Meriam

39932413R10022

Made in the USA
San Bernardino, CA
07 October 2016